I0649642

OJIBWE STYLE MOCCASIN GAME :

Makazinataagewin

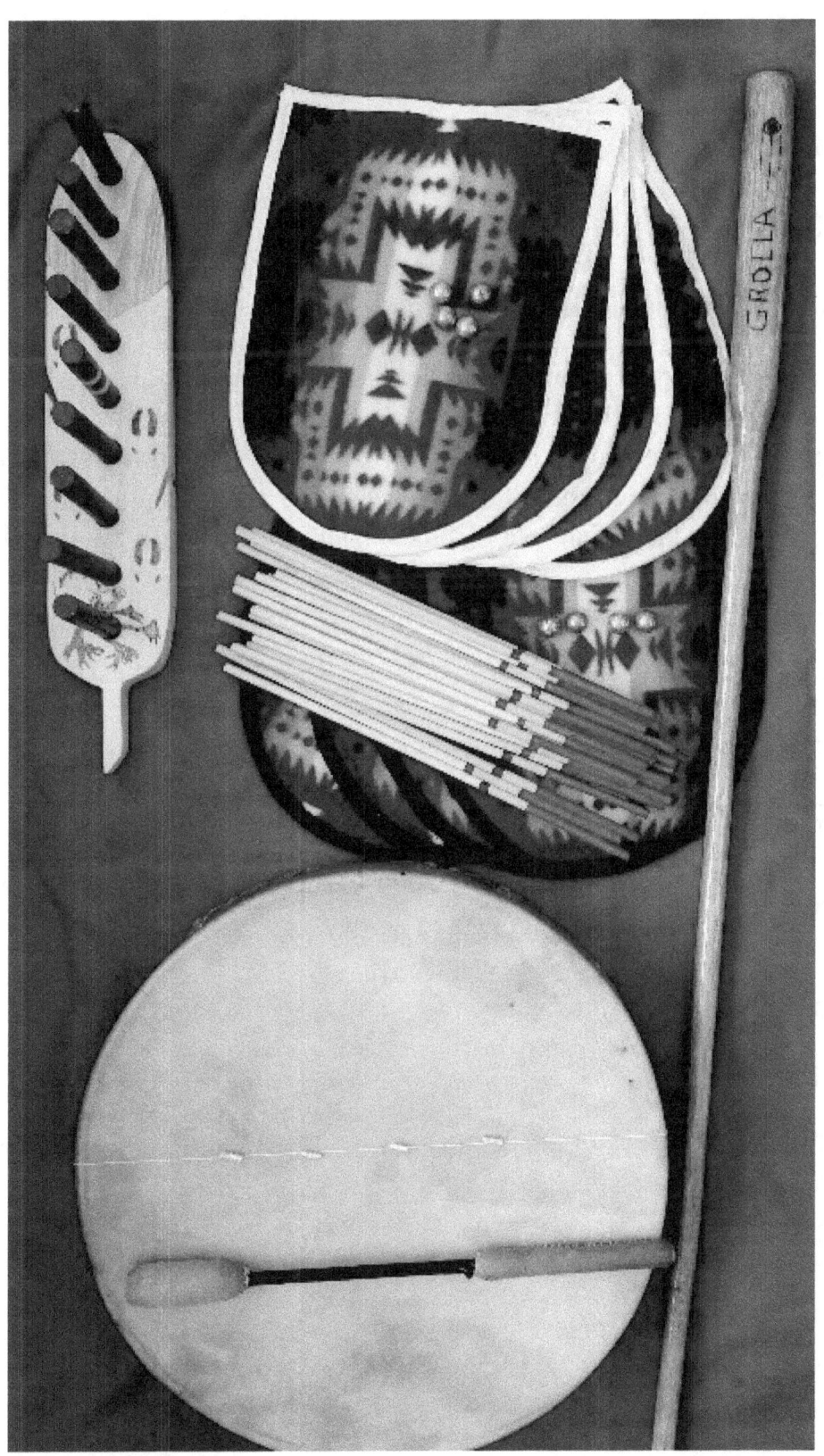

Photos and Diagrams by Charles Grolla

First Edition

Makazinataagewin

Copyright(c) 2017 by Ogimaagiizhig Odoodeman Adikwan (Charles Grolla)

All rights reserved under International Copyright Conventions. No parts of this book may be reproduced, stored in a retrieval system, or transmitted in any form or by any means (electronic, mechanical, photocopy, recording or otherwise) without the express written consent of the copyright holder and PUBLISHER with the sole exception of the fair use provisions recognized by laws. Fair use includes brief quotations in published reviews.

On File: Library of Congress

Grolla, Charles (1972 –)

OJIBWE STYLE MOCCASIN GAME | Makazinataagewin

ISBN-13: 978-0692851906 (Blue Hand Books)

PUBLISHER: Blue Hand Books, 442 Main Street #1061, Greenfield, MA 01301, www.bluehandcollective.com or www.bluehandbooks.org

EMAIL: bluehandcollective@outlook.com

Printed in the USA

REFERENCE | Anishinabe Ojibwe Chippewa | History | Moccasin Game Ojibwe Style

I would like to dedicate this book to the Ojibwe men that took the chance and kept the beautiful game of moccasin game alive during the assault on Ojibwe language and culture.

Contents

Foreward

Boozhoo (Greetings).

If you are reading this I want to say thank you, because the more people that learn and play moccasin game the better the chances are of this beautiful game surviving and being passed on to the next generations of young men.

Before you read on through this booklet I would like to take a little bit of your time to tell you how this booklet project developed.

First I want to say I do not know everything about Ojibwe style of moccasin game. There are Ojibwe men out there in our Ojibwe communities that have been playing longer than I have and they might even have a different way of explaining this game. They might know things about the game that I do not and those ideas, concepts, and knowledge might not be mentioned in this booklet. I do not claim to be the only person with moccasin game knowledge and I am not the only expert, there are many others throughout Ojibwe country.

While growing up in the West End area of the Red Lake Reservation where my learning of moccasin game first took place, there were many men who played this game and played it all the time. I heard the Ojibwe language being spoken almost daily. This was in the early 1980's and I never intended on being a teacher of either the language or the game of moccasin. I never dreamed there would be a need for teachers of either moccasin game or the Ojibwe language. Currently in the area of West End you do not see anyone playing moccasin game in the summer, you do not hear the faint sound of Ojibwe language being spoken at the neighbor's house or anyone communicating in the language of our ancestors. I figured moccasin game and the Ojibwe language would be passed on from one generation to the next without any troubles. It was not until about 8 years before I am writing this that I noticed that my generation was not using the Ojibwe language and moccasin game was being played less frequent. There were no longer any moccasin game practice sessions like the ones that took place back in the 1980's. The many moccasin game tournaments that I enjoyed all through Ojibwe country were no more. There were maybe two moccasin game tournaments yearly in my area and those were in Roseau River Manitoba and Red lake Minnesota. During the 1980's there were several yearly moccasin game tournaments throughout northern Minnesota, Manitoba and Ontario Canada.

Now that I teach this game, mainly in the high school classroom setting, I feel the teaching and learning of the game has changed. I learned the game by observing it for a few years before I started to play and that was only when I was given an opportunity to sit in and play for a player who could not continue to play with his team one evening because he became ill. I started with the easiest and less complex of the playing positions on that team that night. I went on to master that position then I went to the next position until I knew all positions and the major aspects of the game. This took time and did not happen overnight, it actually took a few years of playing regularly. Once I and my brother could play a full game without any guidance from older players we formed our own team and 30 years later we still play for the most part with the same team members as we did back then. Learning the game like this is no longer the case. The students that I have taught, have learned to play from me showing them the whole game for a class period a day and sometimes two class periods certain days of the week.

This is when I started creating this booklet. I wanted to create something in writing that my students could use in my absence to play the game correctly. This goes against the grain of the traditional way of teaching this ancient game. I consulted elders before writing and documenting this game and asked them for permission to do this. I was advised that times are changing and the traditional way of learning our age old legends, sacred teachings, sacred ceremonies, and cultural ways are no longer the same. I was advised to do whatever it took to show these students this sacred game because they would not get this information and exposure anywhere else. I was given permission to write things down.

At my volunteer group I teach the game once a week, young and old men alike attend and have learned the game. These men would attempt to play on their own and when you are just learning this complex game it is hard to remember the rules and procedures. There are not as many players as there used to be and they would rely on a phone call to me or to have someone to be there that knew the game. This was hard and many learners of the game would get discouraged and confused. This is another reason I wrote this booklet so they could get through a full game without having to call or having to have a master player present to complete a game. I felt the need for this and once I developed this booklet I used it in my high school classes and with my group members as a resource. I now feel this to be an asset to the game and feel I need to share it with whoever is interested in learning and playing the game. This is why I have decided to publish this booklet and make it accessible to everyone who is interested and who may be able to use this booklet.

I encourage anyone who finds inconsistencies, problems, or knows a better way to write this age old knowledge down to do so for the survival of this beautiful game. There is a need for teaching resources for moccasin game and the Ojibwe language and culture. My goal as I wrote this teaching aid for myself was to lock in what information I know about this game. Also another reason, if the game were to die out and does not survive, an Ojibwe child 150 years from now could take this booklet and revive this game and at least come close to playing the game of what it is now and lasts as long as the world lasts.

I must warn, this game will not be learned in one sitting or in several sittings. It takes time and energy and you have to play this game to learn it. I have noticed that since I have been teaching moccasin game that there is a common belief among people that do not know the game. They think automatically that this game is an easy guessing game for kids. Don't be fooled, this game is for young men and men, it is a complex game as you will see.

Again, I thank you for taking interest in the beautiful game of moccasin and I hope you enjoy what I have come to enjoy from this game and find this booklet useful.

– Ogimaagiizhig Odoodeman Adikwan (Charles Grolla)

1

Introduction

Moccasin game is a men's game, traditionally, played by men only. This game is played by hiding four marbles under four moccasin pads, and in former times, used moccasins that could be worn. One of the marbles is marked or differently colored than the other three.

Shooting sticks made of oak are used to make the guesses. Twenty counting sticks, made of thin wooden dowels about a foot long, are used for the counting. Nine smaller sticks, three inches long and as thick as a thumb are also used for the scoring. These smaller scoring sticks are called soldiers or Zhiimaaganish. Two to three men or young men make a team. Two teams play each other and will sit across from each other on a blanket laid on the floor or ground. One teammate will hide the marbles while one of the others pounds on a drum and sings. The beat used to pound the drum is unique to moccasin game and sounds like a horse trotting. The opposing team guesses the location of the marked or different colored marble. For each attempt at finding this marked marble, the team pays a certain number of counting sticks which leads to scoring a soldier or small scoring stick which then leads to winning the game. Usually the first team to collect five soldiers or scoring sticks wins the game. Once the marked marble is successfully located, the hider is paid what he is owed in counting sticks and then the opposing team's hider hides his marbles. This goes back and forth until one team attains the five soldiers and wins the game. A game can last several hours or one hour at the least. A tournament usually starts on a Saturday afternoon plays into the night and resumes Sunday morning and lasts all day with the championship game getting over during the evening. Some bigger tournaments start earlier and last three days.

There is one other variation of this type of moccasin game. There is an Ojibwe style that we are playing here and a Dakota style. Ojibwe style moccasin game is still played on the Red Lake, Mille Lacs, Nett Lake, White Earth, Leech Lake, Roseau River, and Lac La Croix Reservations. Moccasin Game tournaments are conducted during the pow-wows and celebrations of their reservations. There are regional differences in rules but they are minor. Teams travel from reservation to reservation to participate in tournaments.

The Ojibwe style of moccasin game presented here is of my understanding and what I learned about moccasin game as I grew up playing this beautiful game, mainly on the Red Lake Reservation. There are minor differences in rules in different Ojibwe communities and what I am presenting in this book are rules of the Red Lake and Nett Lake reservations in Minnesota.

As I understand it, moccasin game had almost become nonexistent for a period of time and was almost nonexistent for several years before a few elders started to bring the game back and volunteer their time and energy to teach the younger generation the moccasin game. I was lucky to be in the midst of this era of teaching the moccasin game and was able to play with many elders in a few different communities through the years. We played in these areas: Mille Lacs Lake Reservation, Minnesota; Roseau River First Nation, Manitoba; Red Lake Reservation, Minnesota; Fort Frances, Ontario; and Brandon, Manitoba.

My early years of learning the game were in the time before there were all the video games. After school, I, along with several friends, would get together and play moccasin game through the evening and late into the night, sometimes all weekend. We would travel to different moccasin game tournaments around Ojibwe country and participate. Probably our oldest Ojibwe men's game, moccasin game has been and is still a big part of our Ojibwe culture even to this day. Every Ojibwe community has stories of when moccasin game was played a lot and at all kinds of occasions. A lot of the older elders taught us how to play and these were the guys we played many games against; many are gone into the next world now and are probably playing moccasin game over there. I have a deep appreciation to our elders for passing this awesome game on to my generation and I feel it my duty to pass on the moccasin game also.

There are many teachings in the moccasin game for our native male youth of today. The game teaches good competition between men and how to work as a team and teaches about one's self and gives a sense of identity as Ojibwe. It is a good social event for men to be around other men and like my longtime friend Todd said, it gives men a sober social environment to get together and teach our young males about being men. The moccasin game is said to have a power that heals its players and keeps them in good health and keeps them out of trouble. I believe this to be true. The old guys I learned from lived to be a good old age and were pretty much healthy and seemed to return to the moccasin game tournaments every year.

The first time my brother and I taught the game as a class, it was to a group of at-risk male youth and while they were meeting with us regularly they stayed out of trouble. The moccasin game for me has been a valuable tool in changing the issue of our youth not knowing their identity and what it is to be Ojibwe or Native American. Teaching them who they are and what are our own traditions of being a man leads to a betterment of all. This game is at least a thousand years old, if not thousands and has been used that long for just this purpose, and being an enjoyable social event. These are just a few of the reasons and teachings surrounding moccasin game and its purpose and spirituality.

2

Origin and History of Ojibwe style Moccasin Game

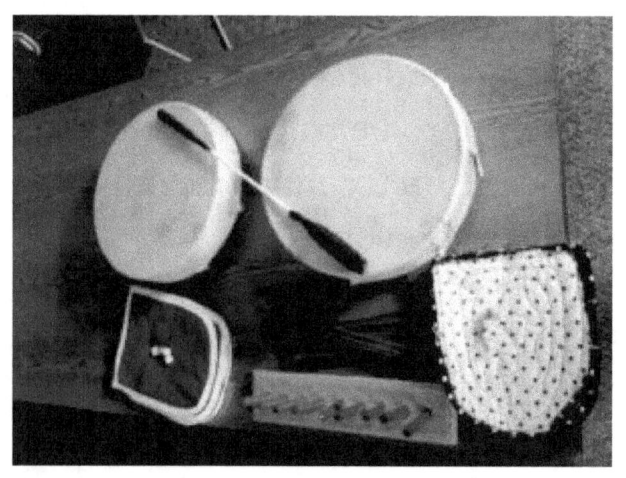

Let me start by saying moccasin game is a men's game and is traditionally played by men only.

The Ojibwe people speak the most complex language in the world and like their language, Moccasin game is a complex game and it is said that the only way to truly learn the game is to play it. The Ojibwe word for the game is Makazinataagewin, pronounced (moccasin ah taa gay win). There are two styles of moccasin game, Ojibwe style that is presented in this book and Dakota style that is similar but less complex and is played by the Dakota that border the Ojibwe.

In former times moccasin game was played for anything and at any time. With the assault on language and culture of the indigenous peoples by the

United States government the church labeled moccasin game a gambling game and outlawed it. The game went underground and survived but still carries the negative stigma of being a gambling game. Sometimes wagers are made on moccasin games but I see more wagers being made on professional sports, college sports and high school sports than I do on moccasin game. As you will see as I explain the origin of the moccasin game, it is a beautiful game and is the exact opposite of what it was labeled in the past by the dominant society, missionaries, Government agents, and the Bureau of Indian Affairs. I am thankful that the moccasin game lived on and thanks to the many Ojibwe men that took the risk and kept it alive.

The origin of the moccasin game is a very old legend and is considered a sacred story.

I travelled one cold winter evening to formally request an elder relative to share this sacred story with me. This elder relative is the only known person that I know of that possesses this sacred knowledge at this time. It is our way to give a gift of tobacco, a gift (usually a blanket), and nowadays some money to request sacred information and can only be done in this manner. After travelling a long distance I was greeted with some really good Ojibwe hospitality. In a respectful and sacred way I gave my gifts starting with the tobacco and made my request. This elder told me in the English language that he could only tell me this sacred story in the Ojibwe language. This elder then switched to Ojibwe without a flinch, smoked his sacred pipe and shared this lengthy sacred story that I am now going to share with you in English and translate the best I can to English. Keep in mind that nothing can really be translated 100% to English from Ojibwe because the world views, cultures, language, societal norms, and way of thinking are very different. Also, my version might differ from other accounts of this already documented legend.

A very long time ago, long before the time of the coming of the white race to Turtle Island (North America), there was an Ojibwe man who lived his life as Ojibwe did in those times. He lived in a village with other Ojibwe and he had a wife and two kids. They lived the normal Ojibwe life and enjoyed it. There came a time when the man's wife and two children died and passed to the next world. The man became stricken with grief and gave up his daily routines and quit taking care of himself. The man became very depressed that his wife and children were gone. People would come and try and talk to the man and help him with his grief but he did not listen and his condition worsened. One day he left the village and went far out into the woods. The man walked and walked and became weak from not eating; his clothes were becoming raged and hung on him as his condition worsened. The man kept walking and got as far away from his village as he could, going ever deeper into the forest. The man was very deep in the forest and when animals would see his condition they would take pity on the man; they would attempt to give themselves to him for food and clothing but the man would refuse their sacrifice and would just keep walking. Once a deer took pity and stood still until the man was almost touching him and the man walked around the deer not accepting the deer's generosity. His body and cloths were deteriorating as he journeyed ever further and deeper into the wilderness. As he walked into a clearing he fell to his knees from exhaustion and was hunched over. Just then he heard someone approaching. As the person walked up to his side, the man thought to himself, I hope it is an enemy warrior that will take my pitiful life and I will not be miserable anymore. This person that walked up asked him what was wrong. The man answered, I have lost my wife and children and I do not want to live anymore, kill me or leave me alone. The man while hunched over and on his knees turned his head to see the man and he did not recognize him. The man was carrying a sack draped over his shoulder. The man carrying the sack helped the ill man to sit up and said to him, I will show you something; it is a gift from me to you. It is a game that you will take back to the people and it will make you feel good and lift your grief and it will draw people together when you play it. It is a healing game and it will take care of you and those that play the game. It is a men's game and although it will not replace your wife and kids, it will bring back those good feelings and laughter that you once had when your family were with you. The ill man accepted and this man fed the ill man some berries, fish, and tea that he had. The ill man consumed the nourishing gift and began to feel better.

The man took the sack from his shoulder and opened it. There were several items in the sack and the man began to take them out one by one and place them on the ground in front of the ill man. The man took out the moccasins and laid them down four in a row, then he took out the counting sticks and placed them on the ground, then took out the short sticks also called soldiers, then he took out the marbles: one different and three the same, then he took out the shooting stick and it measured from the tip of his middle finger to his shoulder: the length of his arm. The last item that he took from the sack was the hand drum and drum stick. The man showed him the drum beat to be used for moccasin game and said there would be songs, many songs that would be sung and used for this game. He then showed him how the game would be played, the scoring of the sticks and the games procedures. After he explained the game to the man, he put the game back in the sack and gave it to the ill man. When the man left he walked towards the woods and took four steps and looked back at the man and the ill man saw that from the knees down he had black fur. The man took another four steps and from the waist down turned into black fur, then another four steps and from the shoulders down turned to black fur, then another four steps and stopped at the edge of the clearing and his head turned to black fur and the ill man saw that he turned into a Black Bear. This man that gave him the moccasin game had turned into a Black Bear and ran off into the woods and ill man realized that something spiritual had just happened and he then knew this is a very sacred game to be shared with the people. This is why the game was called the Bear game before it was called the moccasin game of our time.

During the spring ceremony called the Bear Smoke, the Bear is given thanks for the moccasin game and the healing and medicines the Bear Brings to the people.

A similar legend that originated in the Bois Forte (Nett Lake) community.

This is a story that was shared with me from a relative of mine that resides in the Nett Lake village on the Bois Forte reservation in Minnesota. This is a story that was documented by a visitor long ago to the Nett Lake village who inquired the origin of the moccasin game and a community member obliged. This story deserves mention and as a part of this book and history of the moccasin game.

It was not Nanaboozhoo who created the moccasin game, it was after Nanaboozhoo had created everything; it was an Ojibwe boy who had fasted for ten days and was gifted by a Bear. The Bear gave the boy instructions on how the moccasin game would be played and he was told that the game would last as long as the world would last. The Bear said that in the daytime people should not play and only play when dark. The Bear showed the boy the moccasin's that would be used, four in a row and this represented the Bear's four paws. The Bear gave instructions on how the game would be played and gave caution to what players wagered in the games. The Bear instructed the boy to make a bow and arrows and once completed to announce to the people the coming of a new game. Then gift four boys of his choosing the bow and arrows and tell them the instructions of the game, then those four boys will live out the full span of their lives. They will gain the spiritual power of the game. The Bear told the boy, "You will put this gift of the game and your long life to good use. Now break your fast and remember what I said and take this gift to the people."

The boy broke his fast and when he arrived home he told his father (his father was an ordinary Ojibwe man), "I want to tell you about a game. I have been gifted something by a Bear, I was given a bow and arrows so I could give them to four boys, they will live to an old age and because of that the people will cherish the game and a good life." The father said, "Do not leave this blessing undone, go and complete what you were instructed to do." The boy began at once making the game pieces and the father began to make a special wiigiwaam and was later helped by four boys that would receive the game. The wiigiwaam was completed that afternoon. The boys were anxious for the coming of night and went throughout the village giving invitations to everyone to come and join them and smoke. Evening came and the guests came and started to smoke and behind the fire they saw the game and pondered on what it was. Finally the boy stood and spoke to everyone saying the time has come for you all to see this new game; he placed the two teams facing each other. The boy taught them how the game should be played as the Bear instructed. The moccasins were placed side by side and a ball of fur he hid under the moccasins. The boy then pounded the drum and sang a song that the Bear had sang to him on his fast. The song had words and was translated to saying, "Touch the moccasin where you think the ball of fur is" and this verse was repeated four times. All night they played the game together. Then at dawn they stopped. When it became night again, they played the game all night again. For seven nights they played and then on the eighth night, they finished the first game. The next time they played the game it was seven nights, the boy told the people that this is how the game would be played and this game would never stop being played as long as the world would last. The boy said for unknown reasons the game will be played differently in different areas, but the use of the bow and arrows will continue as long as the world will last. The people will appreciate and deeply respect this game. The players will live to an old age and the Spirits will look favorable upon them and use your tobacco to pay respect to the spirits and don't play the game carelessly.

The Boy and the first four players lived to a very old age and all those who play the game live to an old age and stay out of trouble. The spirits of the game take care of them. This is why the people deem the game very sacred because of the power from the spirits. This was the first men's game of the Ojibwe.

The Ojibwe gifted the Bwaanag (Dakota) with the moccasin game:

My grandmother told a story about how the Dakota were gifted the moccasin game from the Ojibwe. She said there was an Ojibwe hunting party tracking a herd of elk up near present day Roseau, Minnesota, west of the Red Lake reservation. There are still elk herds up in this area to this day. The Ojibwe were getting ready to kill some of these elk and saw that there were other people in the area so they stopped and went to see who was following them. When they went to investigate, they located a party of Dakota hunters that were following the same herd of elk. If they attacked the Dakota hunting party, they would cause the elk to disperse and did not want that, they did not know when they would get another chance at these elk. The Ojibwe made contact with the Dakota and challenged them to a game that they would show them. In this game between the Ojibwe and Dakota hunting parties, their arrows were used as counters and for time's sake they went to one soldier (short stick) and who ever won would make the other hunting party arrowless and the defeated hunting party would have to leave to get more arrows and find a different location to hunt. The Ojibwe showed the Dakota a less complex version of moccasin game and used a pebble to hide under the four moccasins and used a similar count without the Swaasgaan and trapper position (home moccasin). The counting was basic, four and two sticks (arrows). There is debate about who won this first game between the Ojibwe and Dakota hunting parties but it is known that they had parted ways as friends and both parties shared the Elk meat from the hunt and appreciate a better understanding of each other. The Dakota style uses one bead or bullet to hide under their four moccasin pads and their counter sticks are very large, the size of an actual arrow, compared to the Ojibwe counters that are half to one-third the size. The playing pieces of the Dakota style are the same and game set up is the same. The counting /scoring is different; their teams are usually four men per team, counters and moccasin pads are a lot larger.

Moccasin game, White Earth Reservation.
Creator: Robert G. Beaulieu
Photograph Collection, 1920
Collections Online | Minnesota Historical Society
Location No. E97.38 r3 Negative No. 7571

3

Moccasin Game Equipment and Nomenclature

 **A set of Moccasin game pads.** One set for each team. One set at the least will do. In former times moccasins that were worn, were used. Nowadays moccasin game pads are used. There are the rounded top moccasin game pads and the square style moccasin pads. Both are used regularly and the size depends on the hider's preference. Moccasin pads are usually 12 inches long by 10 inches wide, give or take an inch or two. Some moccasin pads are very large and some just big enough to get ones hand under and hide a marble or bearing.

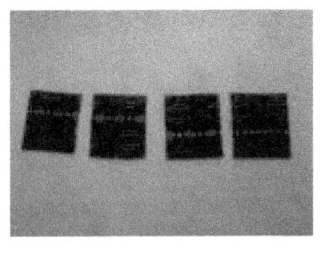

* Note: the moccasin pads that are rounded on the top and bottom are made like this to resemble the shape of the Bear's feet (right).

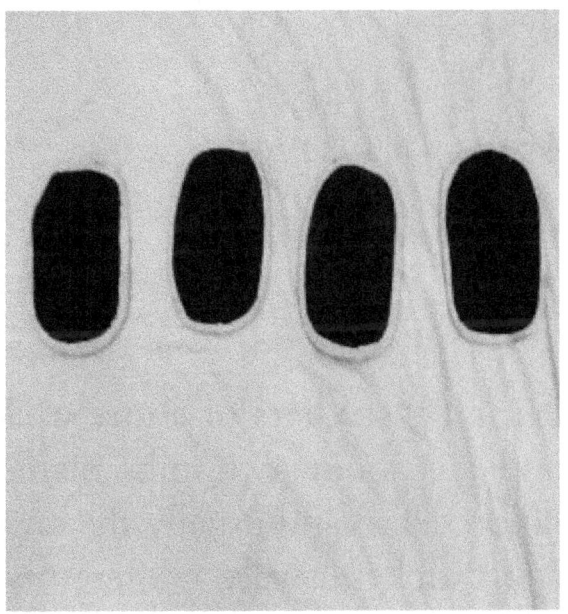

Twenty (20) counting sticks. These sticks, usually a wooden dowel, and are usually about 12 to 14 inches long and about ¼ inch in diameter. These are used for counting and are usually called counting sticks and can be painted any desired color.

Counting Sticks

These sticks are said to represent arrows.

short sticks

Nine (9) soldiers or short sticks. These sticks are about 3 to 4 inches long and are about a thumbs diameter, around 5/8 inch. These sticks can be colored also and usually the same color as the counting sticks. The one odd short stick is usually a differently marked stick signifying the winning point. This odd short stick could be decorated. These short sticks or soldiers can be set in a board that lays flat on the floor and the short sticks or soldiers stand up straight showing players and observers what the score is for each team.

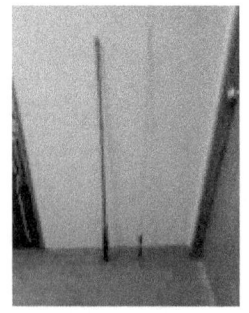

Shooting sticks. Each team should possess a shooting stick. It can be carved out of oak and stained or just a stick from the brush or it can be a fiberglass horse whip or a reflector rod from a reflector from the end of the driveway. In any case, the shooting stick is usually 3 ½ to 4 ½ feet long and is used to reach across the playing mat to flip and strike moccasin pads. Before there was an abundance of fiberglass rods available, these shooting sticks were carved out of oak. There was a lot of time and work put into these shooting sticks and they became beautiful pieces of work. The older players used these carved wooden shooting sticks. It seems the more serious players, especially those that have played the game for a long time, use the carved oak shooting sticks. See more on the old time shooting sticks in chapter 17.

Set of Bearings or marbles. Each team should have at least one set of marbles or bearings each. Three of which should be the same and one different, either by color are physically marked. Glass marbles are the easiest to acquire but are easily seen by the opposing team and experienced hiders usually prefer metal ball bearings like the kind from a CV joint from a vehicle. Then they are marked; one of four is marked using a grinder. The style I prefer and grew up with, as sort of the nicest bearing to use, is a brass ball bearing about 5/8 inch. Brass is easily marked with a vice grip and a metal or wood file. Brass bearings are the nicest ones to have and were highly valued by the older players of my time and are still highly prized. I use a set of brass bearings now that were my deceased uncle Earl's. At his funeral, my mother gave out his moccasin game items to the male players in the family (this is customary). I and my brothers, also our cousin Larry, received his playing pieces and his games. I have a set of his moccasin pads, set of brass bearings, an old time carved oak shooting stick and his game bag. I use these items often when I play and when I teach the game to beginning players. When you have been gifted with a deceased player's game pieces, it is good to talk about the person that once played with those moccasin game pieces when you use them.

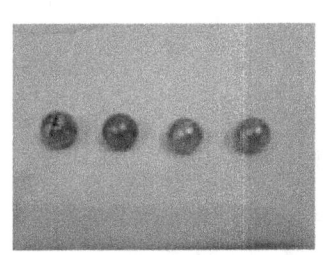 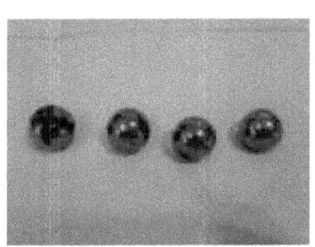 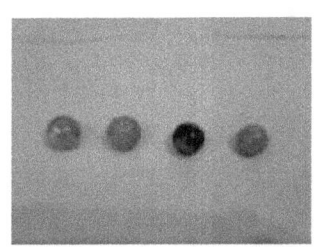

Any kind of marbles or bearings can be used as long as three (3) are the same and one (1) is different, either by color or by having markings on it. I once played in a tournament as a young man and a guy I teamed up with did not have any marbles or bearings, so he used three acorns from a nearby White Oak tree and colored one of them with a permanent marker. We won 5th place in that tournament that had seventeen (17) teams. The brass bearings or metal bearings are preferred because they do not stick to your hands when your hands become sweaty and when hiding you can feel the grooves marked in the marked bearing and you do not have to look to see which moccasin you put it under or remember where it is in your hands, you can feel for it. Remember that only one bearing / marble are hid under each moccasin pad. A person's bearings or marbles that they use regularly are considered good luck to the person using them and are a personal and usually do not let anyone else use them. It is kind of a personal thing and usually only close friends or close relatives will let each other use their personal bearings or marbles. A moccasin game player will always have his prized bearings or marbles in his immediate possession. In former times actual bullet projectiles were used, the round ball musket shot was used in place of bearings and marbles. I understand and was told by a now deceased elder that the brass and metal bearings replaced the musket shot and bullets for moccasin game. I have a friend that I grew up playing moccasin game with that uses four muzzle load bullets and pounded one with a hammer to deform it. This is his personal set and uses them when he plays. You get the idea here, three (3) the same and one (1) different: bearings, glass marbles, bullets, or acorns.

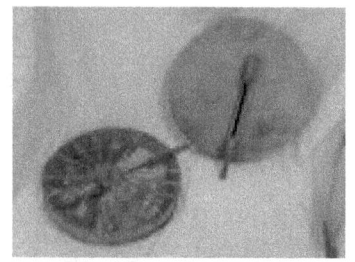

Hand Drum

Hand drum. Each team should have a hand drum, size and shape does not matter and personal preference is usually observed with teams. The hand drum can be one sided or two sided, whatever a person prefers and has handy. Moccasin game songs can be sung but are not a must. These songs are becoming few and not many players sing the songs one sung not so long ago. These songs are usually very personal and certain regions of Ojibwe country have a few distinct songs of their area. The drum is very important to the game; it was said by elders it is not a real game without the drum pounding. The beat is a double beat, one hard and one soft, that is unique to moccasin game and sounds kind of like a horse trotting. An elder once told me that the drum beat for moccasin game was also used for Ojibwe marching into battle. While entering into battle that a singer would run ahead and sing a song using the moccasin game beat.

* Note: One teaching with the moccasin game drum is if a drum is shared between two teams playing each other that when the drum is exchanged between them, it should be rolled to each other across the mat or blanket to show respect for the game and the drum being used.

A blanket or mat. When playing outside in the summer time on the ground, one can get by playing on a blanket. When playing indoors, usually in the winter time, a light mat like the ones used in a gym environment are the best or a couple blankets could be laid on a hard floor or a carpet could be played on also.

I keep a couple of thin quilts to play on. Anywhere you have enough room to lay a blanket down, you have enough room to play moccasin game.

4

Game Set Up

U sually when playing outside in a nice spot, in the shade of a nice tree, a pavilion or lodge, a blanket is laid down, using a standard size blanket is good. When playing indoors and blanket is good but a thin mat with a blanket on it is preferred and the area used is usually 4×6 to 5×7 feet but does not need to be exact.

The hider is always sitting cross-legged or kneeling in the center of his team and the shooter is to his right or left side, as is the marble watcher. If a fourth and fifth player are on the team, they sit directly behind the hider, shooter and marble watcher. The hider is always sitting or kneeling on the ground and the rest of the team sits in chairs but can sit on the ground like in the old days if they want. The teams face each other with the blanket or mat surface between them used as the playing area.

The game scene set up: Overview of game area:

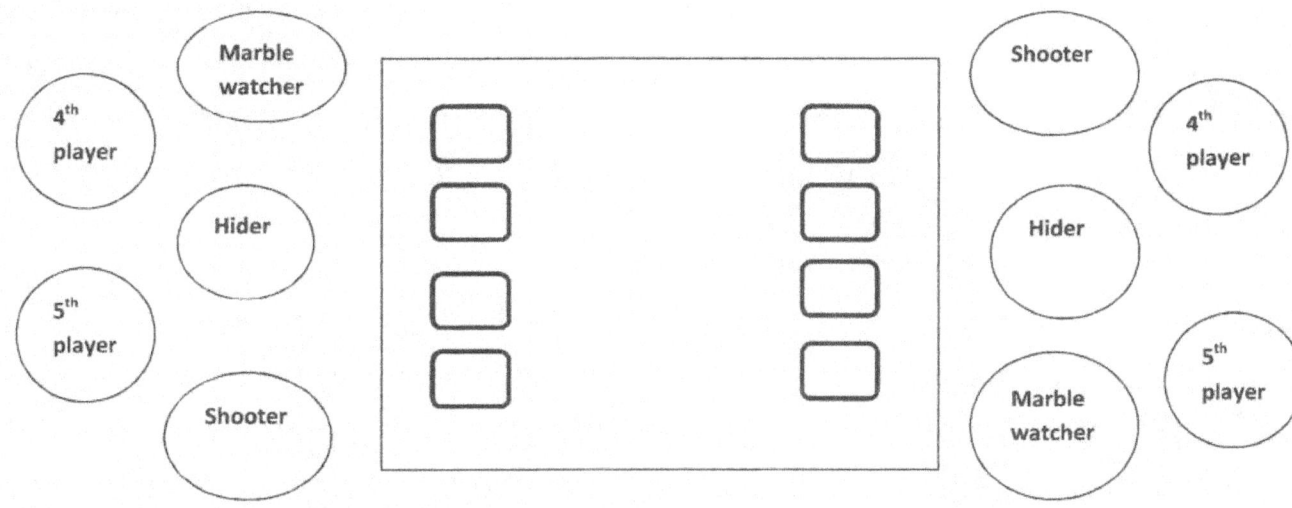

A team can have a minimum of two players and maximum of five players. This would be the team set up and the positions. In the case of a two- man team playing, the hider would be doing the shooting or watching marbles, meaning the hider would be either the shooter or marble watcher. There is the rule that a game cannot just stop and continue playing later, like taking a break. If a team leaves or players leave and they do not have enough players to play and keep the game going, they forfeit the game and lose. If a two-man team cannot sit and play a whole game without having to use the bathroom or getting something to eat then you had better have a third, maybe fourth player. In former times the games went longer, a lot longer than today's tournament play, and players needed to use the bathroom, eat and in extremely long games a player would curl up behind his team and sleep. So since the tournament era started a two-man team can get by. I have been to a couple tournaments where they do not let a two-man team play, it is three, four or five players.

With this overview you can see how the players interact playing the game. You can see how the shooter would reach across the mat with his shooting stick and flip and strike his opponent's moccasin pads. Also, all players but the hider can sit and usually do sit in chairs. But all can sit on the ground or floor if they choose too.

There is a strict rule that **no player is too lay down during the game.** This is seen as very disrespectful to the game and this rule is strictly enforced by tournament judges and elders. The case of a game going for days long was the only exception of lying down and was to sleep for a short time directly behind one's team.

Moccasin game is a gentlemen's game and is respected and treated as such. The game teaches us to win and lose with dignity and without much teasing or badgering a team. Good sportsmanship morals apply. A hand shake between players and teams is a must: tournament judges and elders make sure this happens. This game is very fun and it is a nice social environment for all ages of men to not only play the game but visit, learn, and teach the game. The game is respected and is serious but it is also fun and there is a lot of laughing and joking.

When a hider hides his marbles under the moccasins, he will subconsciously give himself away somehow some way and it is up to the shooting team to find those cues that give his location away. So, by doing this the shooting team will say things like, "there it is... it rolled out," and use the shooting stick and hit next a moccasin or right in front of it, trying to get a reaction out of the hider. A hider has to be cool under these circumstances and will only get better over time, or some will only get better over time. So remember only when the shooter directly hits a moccasin making a choice, then should the hider reveal the marked marble's location. The hider's partners will help by watching the shooting team's actions and letting their hider know what is a good hit (faking a hit, sometimes called a warning shot) or are they just messing with him, trying to fake him out. New players always fall for the false hits and give a signal... like looking at where he hid the marked marble giving the shooting team a clue. And like I said, only after some time playing, maybe several games with different teams, one will get used to this. The only way to truly learn this game is to play it.

5

Start of the Game

Before the start of the game a coin toss is done to determine which team gets to hide first. This means a coin is flipped in the air and a designated player on a team calls it in the air heads or tails and if the coin is correctly guessed that team starts the game by hiding and if not, the other team starts hiding. Remember the only way to earn counting sticks is to hide and ONLY the hiding team gets to pound the drum. The old guys I learned from said it isn't a game without the drum and a hider should wait to hide his marbles until his team mate starts to pound the drum and sing. Singing is optional, but in all my years of playing a good singer makes a difference.

6

Finding Highs and Swaasgaan (home)

A couple of rules pertaining to flipping and striking a moccasin: It has become the universal rule with all tournaments that when a shooter's stick goes under a moccasin just even a little tiny bit, it is ruled a flip, even if the moccasin was not flipped up and the shooter does not see the marble underneath. And if the shooter's stick touches the top of a moccasin even with the slightest tap, it is ruled as a strike and that is the choice of the shooter. Remember now, if the moccasin has been flipped and then that same moccasin is struck, it means nothing.

When the coin toss has been done and a team starts hiding, the opposing team's shooter at the very start of the game is the only one guessing where the marked marble is until highs and lows are found. Highs need to be found before the marble watcher is in the game. It is better to have the marble watcher in the game so the shooting team has two chances at finding the marked marble instead of one. So, usually the shooter will try to find highs right away and does so by flipping one moccasin pad and striking another so they can find highs as soon as possible. To find highs the shooter must make a complete miss of the marked marble. Meaning the marked marble cannot be under either the flipped moccasin or the moccasin that was struck. If the moccasin with the marked marble under it was struck then the shooting team gets to hide and no payment of counting sticks is paid to the hider. If the moccasin with the marked marble was flipped, the hider is paid four counting sticks and the hider keeps hiding: this is a miss but not yet a complete miss. If the marked marble is under a still covered moccasin, this is a complete miss, and the hider will reveal its location. Now that a complete miss is made you have found highs. So, if the marked marble was located under an outside moccasin then the outsides are highs and insides are lows and if the marked marble is located under an inside moccasin, then the inside moccasins are highs and outsides are lows. When highs are found the hider is paid three sticks and continues hiding. The high moccasins are worth six counting sticks and low moccasins are worth four sticks now that highs are found. Remember, one of the high moccasins are always going to be home or swaasgaan from this point on, throughout the rest of the game.

This diagram will show what highs and lows would look like in either case of highs outside or highs inside:

This would be Highs outside and Lows inside

HIGH	LOW	LOW	HIGH
6 sticks	4 sticks	4 sticks	6 sticks

This would be Highs inside and Lows outside

LOW	HIGH	HIGH	LOW
4 sticks	6 sticks	6 sticks	4 sticks

7

Marble Watcher (Trapper)

Now that highs and lows are found the marble watcher is in the game. The marble watcher's job is to cover home. The marble watcher does this by holding a set of marbles in his hand, left or right, and it is usually preferred by experienced players to use colored glass marbles for watching marbles in one's hand because the color is easier to see than the marked bearings preferred for hiding. The marbles are placed securely into the notches of the fingers near the palm. There are four notches and that is why the Great Spirit gave us them for watching marbles while playing moccasin game. With the marble watcher's arm extended and hand out with the top of the hand facing the floor, the marbles are set to the layout of the opponents moccasin pads and the marked marble is in the location of the designated home or swaasgaan. Watching marbles is also called trapping and this position can be called the Trapper also.

So if the highs are on the outside and the outside left is the home moccasin the marked marble should be in the notch on the outside left notch in your hand. As shown here:

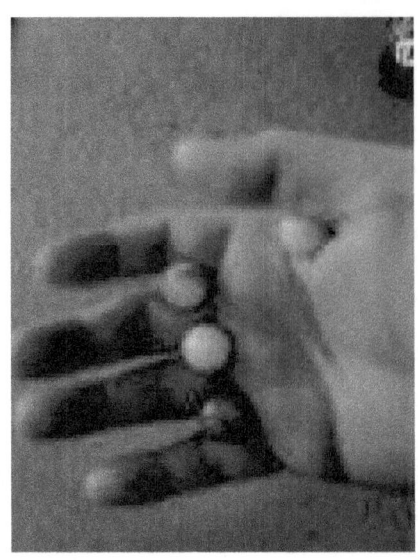

And if the outside right is home the marked bearing would be in outside right notch in your hand. As shown here:

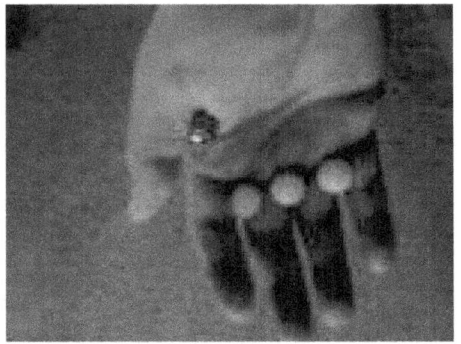

*Remember if you are not at home and have chosen a different moccasin to watch, you are hunting.

8

———

Counting and Earning Counting Sticks

N ow that highs area found and a home is established and the marble watcher or trapper are in the game means that the counting has changed a little. Home is worth 8 counting sticks now and the other high is worth 6 counting sticks and the lows are both 4 counting sticks. This is how the moccasins would look in worth or value of counting sticks:

If highs are on the outside and home is on the left side this is how it would be:

HIGH Home = 8	LOW 4	LOW 4	HIGH 6

If highs are on the outside and home is on the right side this is how it would be;

HIGH 6	LOW 4	LOW 4	HIGH Home = 8

If highs are on the inside and home is on the inside left this is how it would be:

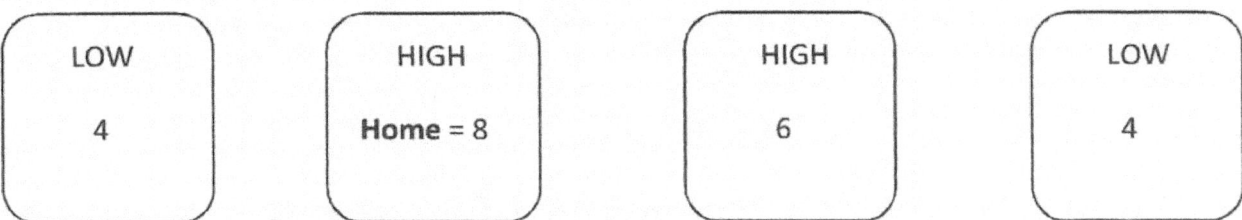

If highs are on the inside and home is on the inside right this is how it would be:

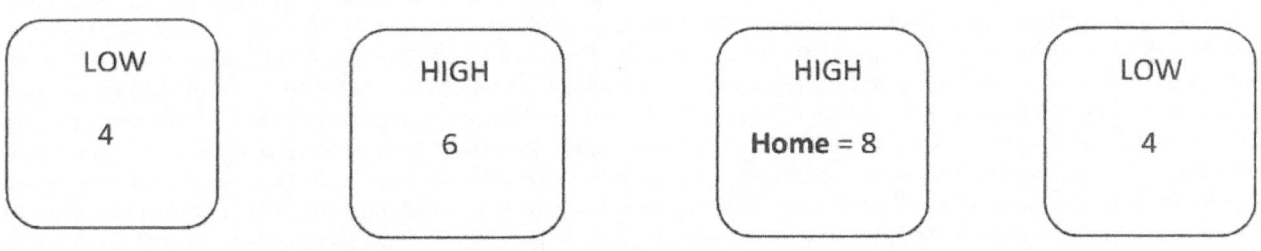

Those are the four different possible outcomes of home. But you have to remember if the shooter forgets where home is or does remember but opens a different moccasin besides the designated home and the marked marble is under the pad, it is still 8 sticks. So remember that… whatever the reason the first flip is always 8 sticks and that is the marble watcher's job or duty to cover that moccasin, and they should coincide with the home moccasin. The marble watcher can hunt when he feels like it but is always taking the chance of paying 8 sticks, also called getting 8 sticked. When the hider deliberately hides the marked marble at home, this is called checking out the marble watcher to see if he is covering home or is out hunting. This places a lot of psychology into the game and is more of a test of wits, trickery and luck when constantly attempting to elude or find the marked marble.

9

How to determine where home (swaasgaan) is on each hide

Where is home located and how is it determined? The home moccasin will ALWAYS be in one of the high moccasins and the last location of the marked marble dictates where home is located for the current hide.

The best way to explain this is to show you this first:

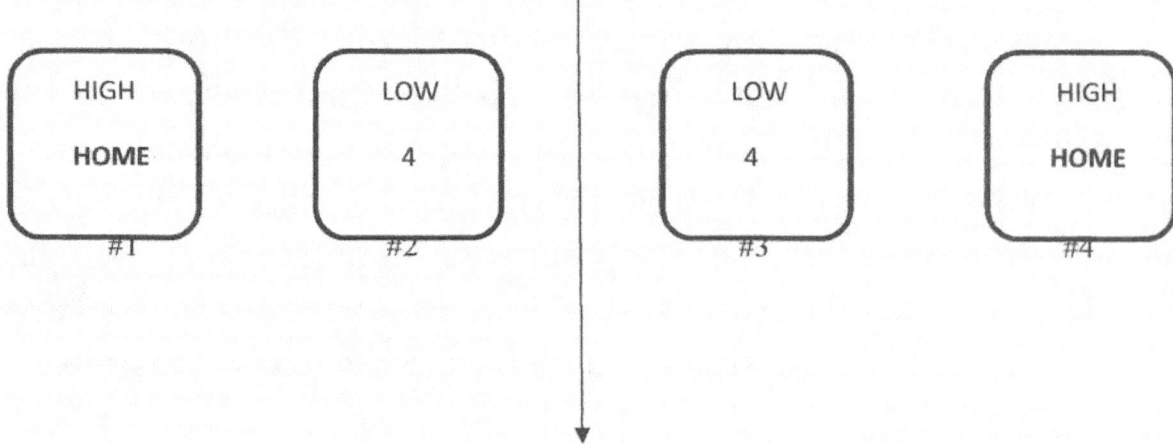

So whichever side it was on the home will be in the high moccasin on that side. So if it was in one of the left side moccasins home will be left side high for the next hide and if it was in one of the right side moccasins home will be the right side high on the next hide. I have numbered the moccasins and put the line between to further clarify how the home is located and the location of home will move to either side throughout the game. The last location pertains to which side of this line the marked marble was on the last hide.

Remember – Home will move from either the #1 to the #4 moccasin always through this game and it all depends on where the hider has hid the marked marble. On the last hide the location of the marked marble was either in the #1 or #2 moccasin's the home will be in the #1 moccasin on the current hide and if it was in the #3 or #4 moccasin's the home will be in the #4 moccasin current hide.

If the highs are on the inside, it would be the inside moccasin that would be home on whichever side the marked marble was located on the last hide.

The shooter and marble watcher need to always be tuned in to the ongoing location of the home moccasin for each hide or play, so they both know which moccasin is home. A slight mistake or miscommunication could cause the shooter to flip the wrong home or marble watcher to be in the wrong home and a flip of the marked marble which would cost a shooting team 8 sticks, maybe a few different times through a game and cause soldiers to be earned by the opposing team. You can see how there is a great deal of psychology in the moccasin game.

There is a lot going on during a game, and if an intense game, you can see how you would have to really concentrate on the game because minor distractions could throw off a player or players and turn the game in a certain team's favor.

OK, now that highs and lows are found and home has been established. Remember that only the hider gets paid and the only exception is if the hider forgets the location of his marked marble and then and only then the hider pays the shooting team 12 counting sticks.

10

Counting sticks – earned and unearned, counted and uncounted (community sticks)

The counting sticks at the start of the game are all uncounted, meaning they have not yet been earned, by hiding, so they are paid out first to the hiders. The count is uniform to the value of the location of the marked marble being under which moccasin pad. Being 8, 6, or 4 sticks and when a successful attempt to find the marked marble has happened, the value is half. If the shooter or marble watcher, only one of them, guesses the marked marble right and the other does not, the hider is paid half of the value. If the shooter and marble watcher both guess the correct location, there is no pay and this is considered a double shot and the shooting team now has to be found twice. So if a shooter opens home and the marked marble is there and the marble watcher is also there in his hand… the value would be 8 sticks, but since the marble watcher got him, the pay is half, 4 sticks, and the shooting team now gets to hide.

When the marble watcher is in the game, a signal is used to notify the other players of both teams that the marble watcher is ready. The marble watcher will signal and does this by either striking a moccasin stick (shooting stick) on the mat or by slapping his forearm and holds his hand with the marbles in it extended out towards the hiding team remaining still and silent until the moccasin he has marked is either flipped or the hide is over by the shooter picking one of the moccasins. If the marble watcher has the correct location of the marked marble, he immediately notifies the hider by signaling again by slapping his forearm and showing the hider his marbles in his hand that he got him or by slapping a moccasin stick on the mat and showing the hider his marbles in his hand with the correct location. If the marble watcher was flipped out, meaning the shooter has flipped home and the marble watcher is there but the marked marble is not or the marble watcher is out hunting and the moccasin he had selected is flipped, in either the case, the marble watcher pulls his hand back, signaling that he is out and the shooter is on his own.

11

Rules and Conduct for the Marble Watcher (trapper)

There are strict rules surrounding the marble watcher. The marble watcher once set CANNOT talk to the shooter and CANNOT have any communication whatsoever with the shooter, signals, gestures, etc... A team mate can only communicate with either the shooter or marble watcher once the marble watcher is set. The marble watcher once set is to hold his hand out with the top of the hand facing the ground and keep his hand still with no movement until he is either flipped out or the play or hide is over. If the marble watcher is still in the game after the first flip, meaning his marked marble is still one of the un-flipped moccasins, the marble watcher signals he is still in the game by again slapping his forearm or striking the mat with his moccasin stick and remaining still. The marble watcher must do this for every moccasin until the hide is over. Once set, the Marble watcher CANNOT move his hand or open it to see where his marked marble is set at. Once his hand is closed it cannot open back up until he is flipped out or he needs to show the hider he got him. So, if the marble watcher violates any of these rules; opening his hand, moving his hand around, or anything that can be thought of as any way manipulating the marbles in his hand while the hide or play is still going on, the marble watcher is out of the play and only the shooter has a chance to guess the location. That is the penalty: losing the second chance, the marble watcher's chance to guess where the marked marble is. The hiding team will be watching for any mistakes or violations of these rules by the marble watcher and it is their responsibility to call it if they see it, observing any of the violations by the marble watcher.

12

Double shooting | The Double shot

Once highs and lows are established and the marble watcher is in the game and from this point on the shooting team can double shoot. Meaning that one of the team's members can double shoot. The double shot has to be signaled by holding two fingers up like a peace sign with the top of the hand towards the hiding team. The hider is usually concentrating on his hide and does not look up or just might not be watching the shooting team at all, so one of the members of his team will call out saying it's a double shot.

The double shot sign looks like this:

 The double shot is a shot only done by the shooter or a person on the team that is double shooting and uses the moccasin stick to shoot and pick. The eight stick rule applies still so if the first moccasin flipped contains the marked marble, the hider gets paid eight counting sticks and the shooter got eight sticked. If one of the shooting team feels

they are very sure of where the marked marble is they can consult the rest of the team and the shooter will give the OK by giving the moccasin stick to whoever is double shooting. The shooting team should be all in agreement of the double shot. So any of the shooting team's players can double shoot. The up side to double shooting is if you find the marked marble, you get to hide and you don't pay anything to the hiding team that was found and the team that double shot has to be found two times. A marker, anything like a pop bottle or cup will be placed on the playing mat or blanket but off to the side to remind the team that they have to be found two times. After one successful find, the cup, pop bottle or whatever marker is being used will come off the mat or blanket signaling that they only have to be found one more time and they get to hide.

The double shot will make you or break you in a game or match. It is not a must but it is helpful in gaining soldiers to win the game when a team has to be found two times instead of just once, especially when the teams are evenly matched and the hiders are found right away and earn only a few counting sticks at a time.

13

Advanced Counting

So now the game is well under way. The counting sticks are all uncounted and are paid out as the hiders hide and get paid. The uncounted sticks are also called community sticks because they do not yet belong to anyone. Both hiders will have earned sticks in front of them on the playing surface and once the uncounted are all gone and they all have become earned they will go back and forth until one teams gets all twenty and trades it in for a soldier or short stick. Then the counting sticks become uncounted or community sticks again. As the uncounted sticks get down to the lower numbers the counting gets a little more complicated but not much once you understand what happens. So each team has counted sticks and the uncounted has gotten down to 4.

Once down to 4 uncounted, the count would be: If you owe 8 you pay the 4 plus 4 of your earned sticks... If you owe 6 you pay just the 4... If you owe 4 you pay the 4..., If you owe 3 you pay 3 and 1 would be left uncounted... If you owe 2 you pay the 2 and 2 would be left uncounted.

Once down to 3 uncounted, the count would be: If you owe 8, you pay the 3 uncounted plus 4 of your earned sticks. If you owe 6, you pay the

3 uncounted plus 3 your earned sticks. If you owe 4, you pay just the 3 uncounted. If you owe 3, you pay the 3 uncounted. If you owe 2, you pay 2 and 1 is left uncounted.

Once down to 2 uncounted, the count would be. If you owe 8, you pay the 2 uncounted plus 4 of your earned sticks. If you owe 6, you pay the 2 uncounted plus 3 of your earned sticks. If you owe 4, you pay the 2 uncounted plus 2 of your earned sticks. If you owe 2, you pay the 2 uncounted sticks.

Once down to 1 uncounted, the count would be. If you owe 8 you pay the 1 uncounted plus 4 of your earned sticks. If you owe 6, you pay the 1 uncounted plus 3 of your earned sticks. If you owe 4, you pay the 1 uncounted plus 2 of your earned sticks. If you owe 2, you pay the 1 uncounted plus 1 of your earned sticks.

There is a special rule with the 1 uncounted stick. As long as you have at least 3 counted sticks to back it up, the shooting team can double shoot on this 1 uncounted stick and the rule is that if the double shot is successful, the hider must hide again and if that double shot is successful, the hider must again hide, and if that double is successful again, the hider must hide and so on and so on until the shooter misses then the hider is paid for that miss. So, for every one of the successful double shots, the shooting team must be found 2 times. So if the shooter got the hider 3 times in a row before he finally missed, the shooting team has to be found 6 times. So if it was 10 times in a row, he was found, then that team has to be found 20 times. I have only personally seen this happen a few times and the highest was 5 times in a row and they had to be found 10 times. In a game I was playing in last year we doubled on 1 uncounted and got the hider 3 times and we had to be found 6 times. When a team gets down to 1 uncounted, they do not have to double on it, it is by choice, and it is not a must.

The counting of the uncounted and earned are the hardest to remember and there are differences from community to community. This rule in Millacs of paying only the 3 has just changed because it was not the case 20 years ago. In the Millacs Lake area when there is only 3 uncounted left, that is all that is paid, there is no 3 plus 4 or 3 plus 3 or 3 plus 2; it is just the 3 that gets paid.

Also a successful double shot in some areas needs to be followed up on the next hide. For example, if you successfully double shot and after they got you the 2 times and they hid again, you would have to double shoot again automatically but in Red Lake or Nett Lake you would not have to.

14

___

Advanced Counting a defined review

Let's review the possible counts and how they would get paid:

12 sticks: The hider forgot and has to pay the shooting team 12 earned sticks if does not have enough, he pays them as he earns them. So don't forget where you hid the marked marble!

8 sticks: The shooter opened home and the marked marble was there and the marble watcher was not home. The first flip regardless if the marble watcher was in the game or not, and if the shooter forgot where home was located. First flip is always home regardless of where it really is.

7 sticks: The shooter got 8 sticked but only had 3 uncounted so they paid the 3 plus 4 of their earned sticks making 7.

6 sticks: The hider was missed and was in a high moccasin or the shooter got 8 sticked and only had 6 sticks to pay.

5 sticks: The shooter owes 6 or 8 sticks but has only 5 uncounted or the shooter owes 6 and has 2 uncounted and paid 3 of his earned sticks.

4 sticks: The hider was missed in a low moccasin or the hider was missed in the low moccasin and only has 2 uncounted and paid the other 2 out of his eared sticks or the shooter flipped home and the marble watcher was there paying half of 8 being 4 sticks.

3 sticks: The hider is missed in a low moccasin and there are only 3 uncounted left or the shooter or marble watcher successfully found the marked marble under a high moccasin that was not the first flip.

2 sticks: The shooter or marble watcher successfully found the marked marble under a low moccasin.

1 stick: The shooter or marble watcher found the marked marble under a low moccasin and only has 1 uncounted left.

These are all the possible situations for the amount of sticks that could be owed.

When a team gets under 4 sticks, uncounted or counted or a combination of the two, the shooting team only has what is called a single shot. Meaning that only the shooter has the chance to find the hider. And the 8 stick for the first flip still applies. Even when a shooter has a single shot, as long as he does not flip any, and just reaches across and strikes on of the hiders moccasin's making a guess and misses it. The hider should then not reveal the location but tell the shooter to flip a moccasin because the hider still gets his chance at 8 sticks, because they would get a soldier and the counting sticks would turn into uncounted but the hiding team found keeps 4 sticks going into the next soldier.

This single shot has one exception when the shooting team has ONLY 3 EARNED sticks left. So when this happens, and because this is a gentlemen's game, the shooting team will throw over 2 of their 3 earned sticks and signal a double shot. The hider accepts the 2 sticks and allows the double shot, giving the shooting team one last chance to find the marked marble and if he does gets the reward of having to be found twice and saves the soldier by no pay and keeps his 1 earned stick. Thus saving the soldier and getting a good chance to come back.

15

End of Game

Also, when a team is at the point of only having 3, 2, or 1 stick left earned or unearned and the shooter makes a successful single shot, there is NO pay and thus saved the soldier and the shooting team gets to hide and attempt a comeback. So the game or soldier cannot be won by not having enough sticks to pay a regular count. This rule and method is also different depending what area or community you are in. I played a team from up in Ontario Canada one time and when it got down to the last 3, 2, or 1 stick left, they used only two moccasin game pads to hid the marbles and gave the shooting team a 50/50 chance and that's how the game had to be won. So there are differences but the Ojibwe style is basically the same all through Ojibwe country.

16

Changing and Switching Positions

When a soldier is won, this is the only time the players can change positions, like the hider can trade the hiding spot with a team mate, or the shooter can change with the marble watcher and so on. It is not a penalty if the team does not follow this rule but one would have to ask a tournament judge or elder of that area. Most of the time, if both teams are OK with switching positions, whenever they feel like it is OK, but some will insist that it should only be done when the soldier has been earned by either team. One soldier signals one game but the winner of the game is first to 5 or 3 or whatever the agreed upon number is.

Challenges

When a hider is hiding and is being taunted by the shooter or someone on the opposing team and wants to challenge that person to find them, and that person alone, the hider will hide three marbles / bearings leaving the marked one in one of the three and keeping the fourth in his hand… he can take the fourth moccasin pad and throw it at the person who is taunting him and challenge that person. This is then viewed as a double shot. Marble watcher

/ Trapper position is out and the person being challenged is the one who should be shooting. This person that is challenged has to be a member of the opposing team and cannot be someone in the crowd. The pay is regular pay if missed and if the hider is found it is a double shot.

Another challenge is when a short stick or soldier has just been earned and the counting sticks are all uncounted. The shooter will take one (1) stick out of the bundle of twenty (20) and offer the hider the other nineteen (19) sticks. If the hider accepts the nineteen (19) sticks he has accepted the challenge and the shooter will shoot. The marble watcher / trapper is out and the shooter is on his own. If the shooter finds, locates, the marked bearing / marble, the hiding team has to find the shooting team 38 times but keeps the nineteen sticks. If the shooter misses, the hider keeps the nineteen sticks and the shooter pays the hider the one (1) stick and the hiding teams scores a short stick / soldier.

17

The art of making the old style wooden moccasin stick

The old guys I learned the moccasin game from all used a carved wooden shooting stick. This style of shooting stick is considered the old style because of this... the old guys used them all the time. This style of stick is still used today and the serious players that have played for a lot of years usually use a carved wooden shooting stick. It is much easier and faster to go to a store that sells the fiber glass rods for driveway reflectors, horse whips, or long antennas and buy one nowadays but it is nice to have your own carved moccasin stick. Some people will use a simple stick from the forest or an old used fishing pole. Whatever the choice, these moccasin sticks can be and are decorated with colored tape and sometimes bead work and they look very nice or they can be just used the way they are, with no tape or bead work. It is your choice. These old style shooting sticks are a very important component to the moccasin game, as are the pads, marbles and other playing pieces of the game. A serious player always has a complete game which included all the playing items needed: drum, pads, soldiers, counting sticks, blanket, and steal or brass ball bearings and a wooden shooting stick. The stick and bearings are personal items and it is seen as disrespectful to ask someone to borrow them. A team should always show up to a tournament or a game with their own playing equipment.

The old style shooting sticks are made from white oak usually but any type of tree will work. A stick carved from white oak works the best and it is the only kind the old guys used that I learned from back in the mid 1980s. I made one from maple one time and it turned out a nice white color but got dirty easy and I ended up painting it. The maple stick after it dried became very hard and was not as flexible as the white oak sticks are. The white oak stick has a nice natural light brown color and a nice grain pattern. These sticks are carved and are unique to the owner. They can be stained and sealer used on them or just left naturally the way they are.

Here is a carved wooden stick that I carved and a fiber glass driveway reflector rod that I use. The handle on the reflector rod is beaded over the leather handle.

The old style wooden shooting sticks can be made if a player so desires to have one. Here is the process I use that I learned from the late Fred (Freddy J) Jackson, Millacs Lake, and Theodore (Doc) Jones, Red Lake. This is the respected process I learned from these respected elders and legendary moccasin game players around the Red Lake and Millacs Reservations. These two moccasin game legends had each their own distinct moccasin game song that they sang a lot and these two songs are still sung at moccasin game tournaments to this day and are known as Freddy J's song and Doc's song.

It is good to still hear those songs being sung. These old men gifted me with this art of making a moccasin stick and I am gifting you and sharing this priceless knowledge.

First a white oak tree of small to medium size is selected in the forest somewhere. Find a white oak without any branches on the trunk of the tree, at least a 4 to 6 feet section that is limbless is the best. The white oak is cut down and the choice section of the truck is cut out and hauled out to the pick up or where ever it is a good spot is to split it up. The rest of the tree is used for fire wood. This section is then stood up straight usually against the tail gate of the pickup. A flat sided axe and a large hammer are used to split the section of wood. This is usually easier in the middle of winter when the tree is frozen and splits a lot easier. The trunk of the tree is split in half, then the halves are split into halves and so on until you end up with sections of wood about 2 to 3 inches around in diameter. These are now called oak blanks for carving your shooting sticks. The blanks can be saved for working on anytime of the year. The shooting stick can be carved and then dried or the blank can be left to dry out, then carved… what either way works for you. If carved right away and then let dried usually does not have any cracks in it.

Here is a picture of a small white oak trunk split in half:

18

Moccasin Game Terms

Hider: The person who is hiding the marbles under the moccasin game pads. Each team has one hider.

Shooter: The person who uses the shooting stick to flip and strike the moccasin game pads of the opposing team. (Sometimes called the guesser or finder)

Marble watcher: This is the person who holds the marbles in their hand and is their responsibility to cover the home moccasin. The marble watcher is only in the game and has a chance to find the hider after highs and lows are found. (The marble watcher is sometimes called the guard and is also often called the Trapper)

Hunting: Once the marble watcher is in the game and highs and lows have been established it is the marble watcher's responsibility to have home covered and if he is not at home the marble watcher is hunting. You will hear the people say he is hunting after a home is flipped or opened and the marble watcher is not there. There is a penalty for getting caught hunting and it is eight sticks paid to the hider. The marked bearing or marked marble is located in the home moccasin or first flipped moccasin pad.

Eight Sticks: This is when the home is flipped and the marble watcher is not home and can be any of the first flipped moccasins after highs and lows are established, the penalty is eight sticks.

Finding Highs: To find highs, a shooter must completely miss the marked bearing. A complete miss means, it was not flipped or hit and remained covered at the end of the play. If it was flipped, it is four sticks and highs have not been found. If it was struck there is no pay and it is now the shooting teams turn to hide.

Highs and Lows: Designated worth of the moccasin game pads. Four moccasin game pads laid in a row. If the two outside moccasin game pads are highs, they are worth six counting sticks and the two inside moccasin game pads would be lows are worth four counting sticks. And if the two inside are instead highs, then they are worth six counting sticks and that would make the outside pads lows, worth four counting sticks. Whichever they are, highs outside and lows inside or highs outside and lows inside, the high moccasin's are always home or nishwaasigaan, also swaasgaan, and home has the eight stick worth when first flipped.

Home: The home is one of the designated high moccasins always, and is determined after highs and lows are established. The home is the designated high moccasin that the marble watcher is responsible for by having it covered in his hand when the start of the play begins. The location of the marked marble on the last hide dictates the location of the home on the current hide.

Double Shot: A double shot can only be taken after highs and lows are established, highs are found. A double shot means that the shooter has confidence in knowing where the location of the hidden marked marble of the opposing team. The double shot is signaled by a person of the shooting team usually the shooter or striker holding up two fingers, the index and middle finger together with a raised hand or any members of the shooting team who is sure they know the location of the marked marble or bearing.

The shooting team needs to be all in agreement with the person making the double shot, usually the shooter but one of the other shooting team's members can also shoot, if allowed by the rest of his team members who are in agreement. If a double shot is successful in finding the marked marble, it is the shootings team's turn to hide and will have to be found twice. If the double shot is unsuccessful and the flip is revealed on the first flip, it is eight sticks. If it is the second flip or just a miss, the pay is whatever the moccasin is.

Follow up shot: Sometimes after a successful double shot is made and shooter is asked to follow up. Meaning to double shoot again and see if he can correctly guess the location of the marked marble again and this is called following up. This is not mandatory in the Red Lake and Nett Lake areas but is in other areas of Ojibwe country. At the beginning of a tournament this will be mentioned and one can ask if you are playing in another community other than your own. If you do not know about your own area you can as an Akiwenzii (Elder Man) what your community rule is or what it used to be.

Single shot: This is referring to when either there is no highs and lows determined yet or there are not enough counting sticks possessed by the shooting team to keep the marble watcher in play. Single shot is also when the shooting team has either three or two or one counting stick left, either counted or uncounted, or a combination of the two. Under four counting sticks is a single shot unless the shooting team has exactly three counted sticks left in possession and then, and only then, it can be a double shot by throwing over two of the three sticks and the hider accepts them and the shooting team signals a double shot by giving a double shot signal. Also, if the shooter starts by flipping a moccasin pad too early and the marble watcher (trapper) was not ready, has not slapped in signaling he is ready, is deemed a single shot.

The hider forgot where the marble is: The hider is at all times supposed to know where the marked bearing or marked marble is at. To prove that he knows where it is, the hider must acknowledge by signaling when a moccasin is flipped or hit (struck) or chosen by whoever may be shooting. When a choice is made by striking or hitting a moccasin pad by the shooting team, the hider must point to which moccasin the marked one is at and then revealing it to the shooting team as proof he knows where the marked one is hid at. This is a strict rule and failure of revealing the correct location or pointing to the correct moccasin is a big win for the shooting team. The hider must then pay 12 counting sticks to the shooting team. This is the only time a hider pays anyone, a hider always earns counting stick except in the situation when the hider has forgotten where he hid the marked bearing or marked marble while hiding. Hand signals are a must: when a moccasin pad is flipped the hider must signal it is not there by waving his hand, called waving it off, or pointing at it if it is located in that flipped moccasin. If a hider gives the wrong or incorrect hand signal, even if accidental, it is ruled that the hider forgot the location of his marked bearing or marble and owes the shooting team twelve (12) of the hider's <u>earned</u> sticks. When a hider forgets where his marked bearing or marble is the pay is twelve (12) sticks and if the hider was found the shooting team now hides. If the shooting teams missed the shot when the hider forgot, the hider keeps hiding and pays the twelve (12) sticks. The hider is NOT paid for the location of the marked bearing or marble on the hid he forgets the location. This is important to remember. If the hider forgets, he pays the penalty of twelve (12) sticks and this penalty has to be paid with his earned sticks (earned only). This penalty CANNOT be paid from the uncounted. In the case that the hider does not have the full amount to pay 12 sticks, he has to pay as he earns more sticks on his next turns of hiding. The teaching behind this is: that you cannot give away what is not yours.

Uncounted and counted sticks: The long counting sticks at the start of the game are uncounted, meaning they have not yet been earned. These uncounted sticks are sometimes referred to as community sticks because they do not belong to either team yet.   The only other time they are uncounted is when a soldier or short stick is won and all twenty counting sticks become uncounted again and must be earned.   As a hider hides and successfully eludes the other teams shooter and marble watcher, he will earn counting sticks and the uncounted pile is used to pay him with first.   The other team might get the hider and it will be their turn to hide and that hider gets paid from the uncounted as well… this goes on until the uncounted are all gone then the sticks go back and forth until one of the teams attain all the twenty counting sticks and trades them in for a soldier (short stick) and then all twenty become uncounted again and they need to be earned again.   This keeps going until the first team to get five soldiers (short sticks) and they have won the game.

Tournament play and old style of playing: Tournament play is referring to how the soldiers (short sticks) add up to a win.   Nowadays, moccasin game is mainly played at pow-wows and celebrations and that is called tournament play.   It is played in tournament style so that the tournament can be completed in a couple days.   Tournament play means that several teams play each other; a bracket is set with however many teams are registered at the start of the tournament and games are played until all teams have played and been eliminated, leaving it with a first, second, third, fourth place team.   The tournaments are usually double elimination and a team must be beat twice to be eliminated from the tournament.   The old style of playing is referring to the win of soldiers and is usually the first team to get three soldiers in a row or consecutively and wins the game.   So if one of the two teams playing each other wins two soldiers first then the opposing team wins one soldier, the team with two needs to put one soldier back.   If the same team wins another short stick, the other team puts another soldier back and now the score is reversed.   So you can see how this does not fit into a tournament because they would be playing for days and days just like in the old days. They had more time to play back then and nowadays a pow-wow is over in the weekend and the moccasin game tournament needs to be done in that time frame also. You will still see some games for practice play, playing the old style but not as much as you used to see. Every Ojibwe community has old stories about legendary moccasin games being played for very long periods of time, some lasting for a whole day, sometimes two days and sometimes even longer.

19

Tournament Rules

No use of drugs or alcohol while playing in the moccasin game tournament! If you are under the influence or are using drugs or alcohol you will be disqualified from the tournament! Please have respect for our oldest men's game.

- Only males can play. It is a men's game.

- Each team can register two to five players at the start of the tournament and only those players remain on the same team throughout the tournament. No team hopping. No replacements after the team has started their first game of the tournament. If a team mate has to leave or quits, his team can continue provided they have at least two players to continue playing, otherwise they are disqualified and forfeit the tournament. A team cannot get up to leave to go sing or do anything else and come back to play later. A team leaves, they forfeit their game.

- A team will NOT be disqualified if they do NOT have a singer but the drum must be pounded while the game is in play. It is not a game without the drum pounding.

- Area (regional) rules apply except if both teams agree before the start of the game to play their own home (regional) rules.

- Teams are required to have all their own equipment and are responsible to be prepared to play when called upon to play.

- Only ONE marked marble or bearing may be hidden under the moccasins in each turn of hiding. The hider must show the shooting team his marbles before hiding at the start of a game or match. If the hider switches with a team member (new hider) or changes the set of marbles or bearings used, he must show the shooting team what he is using to hide. Showing his new set of bearings or marbles, showing what the marked or odd one looks like. Violation for two or more marked marbles or bearings is disqualification of their team from the tournament.

- When the hider has touched his third moccasin he cannot go back or start the hide over.

- When the shooter has struck and has chosen a moccasin, the hider must point to the location of the marked marble or bearing and then reveal to the shooting team the marked marble or bearing's location. Failure to use hand signals and not revealing the marked marble or bearing's location is ruled that the hider forgot where his marked marble or bearing is and pays the penalty of twelve (12) counting sticks to the shooting team and can ONLY pay with counting sticks he has earned. The hider must use hand signals.

- The shooting team will have _____ minutes to hit a moccasin.

- Hiders must stay in position behind the moccasins until the shooter has completed the play. No sitting in a chair or leaving the hiding area.

- No lying down of any players. It is disrespectful to the game!

- No touching the moccasins with the shooting stick except to strike. If a moccasin is touched, no matter how lightly, or by accident, it will count as a hit. The same goes for a lift of a moccasin, if the shooting stick breaks the plane of the moccasin it is counted as a flip.

- Marble watchers (trappers) must have smacked in by either slapping their forearm that holds the marbles or by striking their moccasin stick on the playing area in front of the team, signaling he is ready. Once this is signaled and the marble watcher is ready and in play there is absolutely NO communication between the shooter and the marble watcher. The Marble watcher must remain still and the slightest movement with his hand holding the marbles makes him disqualified. Violating any of these rules will disqualify the marble watcher for the hide but will be back in on the next hide and the shooter will continue on alone as a single shot.

- The shooter will strike and choose one moccasin ONLY. Hitting two or more moccasins simultaneously when striking will be ruled the first moccasin nearest to the shooter will count as hit.

- No assistance from any non-team members standing around the teams in play. The team receiving the assistance will pay penalty to the opposing team of twelve (12) earned counting sticks and loss of a turn of hiding. The person signaling will be asked to leave the playing area. A second violation the team forfeits the game and is disqualified from the tournament.

- Any disagreement between teams, illegal or unfair play must be reported to the tournament judge (s) immediately and dealt with according to the tournament rules.

- Decisions made by tournament judge (s) are final. The tournament judge (s) will be announced at the beginning of the tournament.

- Double elimination bracket will be used; names of team captains will be drawn to see who plays each other.

- After completion of each game players must shake hands. This is a gentlemen's game.

20

The old guys I learned from

My teachers of moccasin game were all well known in the arena of Ojibwe style moccasin game and some are still talked about at tournaments to this day for relentless double shooting and played games that lasted the longest in recent history, during my lifetime anyway. The gifting me of the moccasin game was one of the best things that has ever happened to me and I cannot give enough thanks to the following legendary moccasin game players who are now passed on:

Charley Geshick (gii-panaash), Bois Forte reservation

Lawrence Geshick, Bois Forte Reservation

John Strong Sr., Bois Forte Reservation

Theodore (Doc) Jones, Red Lake Reservation

McKinley (Mac) Auginash, Red Lake Reservation

Fred (Freddy J) Jackson, Millacs Lake Reservation

Roger (Asiniwinini) White Sr., Red Lake Reservation

Gabe Hayden, Roseau River First Nation Manitoba

Charles (Chucky or Cheesy) Wind, Red Lake Reservation

Lee (Aandeg) Lussier Sr., Red Lake Reservation

Charles (Chubby) Johns

Earl Germolous, White Earth Reservation
and my uncles Merle (Ike) Leecy, Wendell Leecy and James Chavers.

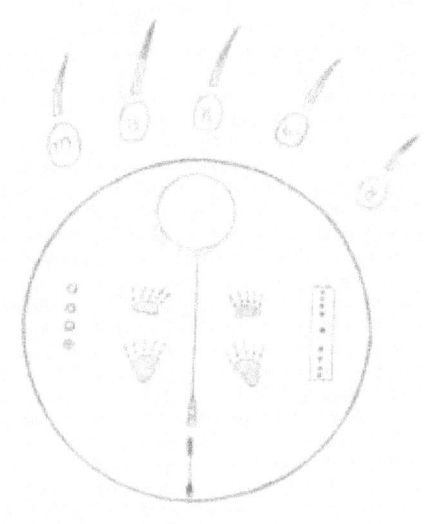

Makwa Drawing by Charles Grolla

Makazinataagewin Ojibwemowin

- Note: double vowel orthography is used here in the writing of the Ojibwe language. Consult the Dictionary of Minnesota Ojibwe by John Nichols or Oshkaabewis Native Journal for double vowel sound charts and how to pronounce Ojibwe vocabulary.

Makazinataagewin – Moccasin game

Makazinataage – S/he plays moccasin game

Nemaabiins (ag) – Marble (s) / Unmarked Bearing (s)

Gaajigan (ag) – Marked bearing (s) / Marked marble (s)

Anwi (in) – Bullet (s), also used for the brass or metal bearings used for hiding

Makazin (an) – Hiding pad (s)

Bashizhe'igan (ag) – Shooting stick (s)

Bima'igan (ag) – Counting stick (s)

Bima'igaans (ag) – Short counting peg (s), also called soldier (s)

Ginwaakwad (oon) – Long Stick (s)

Dakwaakwad (oon) – Short stick (s)

Makazinataage dewe'igaans – Moccasin game drum

Dewe'iganaak – Drum stick

Makazinataage'aawin (an) – Moccasin game pieces

Zhiimaganish – Soldier

Gaadoowinini – Hider

Bashizhe'igewinini – Shooter, also said Baashkizigewinini

Gaajigewinini – Marble watcher or Trapper (Waanii'igewinini)

Endaad – Team   **Endaawaad** – Teams

Ishwaasokaan – Home, moccasin worth 8 sticks, also said Swaasgaan

Ningodwaasokaan – Moccasin worth 6 sticks

Niiyokaan – Moccasin worth 4 sticks

Agindewanan – Counted   **Gaawiin mashi agindesinoon** – Uncounted

Aabiganaa – Single uncounted (with sticks to back it, automatic double shoot until missed)

Niizhoo-bimodan – Double shot, also said Niizh-doono

Niniizho-bimodaa'aa – I am double shooting him

MAKAZINATAAGEWIN OJIBWEMOWIN

Niizho-gabenaage – Score double

Mii iwe dibishkaangwaa – Evened up

Diba'amawishinaam – Pay us

Ogii-mikaan – He found it

Gaawiin gidaa-mikawisii – You are not going to find him

Gwejiwebin owe – Flip it   **Oshtigwaan** – Heads   **Ozod** – Tails

Biisiwebinige – He makes a makes a moccasin game beat (Moccasin game drum beat)

Ombaakwa'an – Lift with a stick

Baakiwebaw – Open him up

Gii-wanichige – Guess wrongly

Wanichige – Make a mistake

Waniike – He forgets

Gaadoon – Hide It

Niwii-pakitewaa Zhiimaganish – I am going to hit the soldier (meaning the marked bearing)

Achige – Place a bet   **Achigewin (an)** – Bet (a wager)

Geyaabi aabiding – One more time

Mizhodam – He hits the target

Niiwezhiwe – He defeats people (in a game or contest)

About the Author

Charles Grolla's Ojibwe name is Ogimaagiizhig (Boss of the Sky) and he is of the Adik (Caribou) clan or totem. He is an enrolled member of the Bois Forte reservation in Minnesota and was raised mainly on the Red Lake reservation in Minnesota. While growing up in the Bikwaakwaang (West End) area of the Red Lake reservation, Charles became a contending player of Ojibwe style moccasin game before the age of 14. Charles graduated from Red Lake High School and completed his Bachelor of Science degree in Criminal Justice with a minor in Ojibwe Language at Bemidji State University. Retiring after 17 years of service from the Red Lake Police Department, first as a police officer then as a conservation officer, he started a new career and is currently a teacher at Cass Lake – Bena High School where he teaches Ojibwe language, culture, and moccasin game.

Charles is a lifetime hunter, trapper, fisherman, and moccasin game player.

As a child, besides moccasin game, growing up his favorite activities were snaring rabbits and helping his family with commercial fishing activities while living a traditional Ojibwe life style. He participated in one of the last Oshki-Ogichidaa (Young Warrior) societies in Red Lake in his youth; this society was founded on living the Seven Sacred Teachings, and used moccasin game as a teaching environment for men, to teach young men how to be positive Native American men. Currently, in addition to teaching high school classes, Charles volunteers once a week to teach moccasin game to the community.

In 2016 Minnesota Indian Education awarded him "Ojibwe Teacher of the Year" for his many accomplishments during his six years of teaching high school Ojibwe language classes.

Charles currently lives in Bemidji Minnesota. You can reach him by email: ogimaagiizhig@yahoo.com

About the Book Cover Photo:

The moccasin game set pictured on the cover was gifted to Charles Grolla from the Northwestern Minnesota Juvenile Center's American Indian Culture group. This game set was fully created by the clients there in 2015. This is his personal game set.

About Blue Hand Books

Blue Hand Books is a non-profit collective of Native American and First Nations authors based in western Massachusetts, founded in 2011.

Our Authors receive 100% of their book royalties.

Facebook: https://www.facebook.com/Blue-Hand-Books

Twitter: @BlueHandBooks

Email: bluehandcollective@outlook.com

Please help us out and tell your friends and relatives about these books. Thank YOU!

Acknowledgements

I would like to thank the these men that supported me always and taught me what it was to be an Ojibwe man: Joe Barret (Joe B), Dewayne Dow Sr., Robert G. Neadeau Sr.(Bob), Donald Desjarlait Sr. (Don Dez), Fred Jackson (Freddy J), Earl Germolus, Lee Lussier Sr., and Dale Johns.
I would like to thank Blue Hand Books for publishing this book.

www.ingramcontent.com/pod-product-compliance
Lightning Source LLC
Chambersburg PA
CBHW080734020726
47503CB00010B/2905